IN PRAISE OF READING
AND FICTION

In Praise of Reading and Fiction

THE NOBEL LECTURE

DECEMBER 7, 2010

Mario Vargas Llosa

Translated from the Spanish by Edith Grossman

FARRAR, STRAUS AND GIROUX

NEW YORK

Farrar, Straus and Giroux
18 West 18th Street, New York 10011

Distributed in Canada by D&M Publishers, Inc.
Printed in the United States of America
First edition, 2011

Library of Congress Cataloging-in-Publication Data
Vargas Llosa, Mario, 1936–
    [Elogio de la lectura y la ficción. English]
    In praise of reading and fiction : the Nobel lecture,
December 7, 2010 / Mario Vargas Llosa ; translated from the
Spanish by Edith Grossman. — 1st ed.
        p.   cm.
    ISBN 978-0-374-17575-7 (hardcover : alk. paper)
    1. Vargas Llosa, Mario, 1936—Books and reading. 2. Books
and reading—Philosophy. 3. Fiction—Appreciation. 4.
Fiction—Authorship.   I. Grossman, Edith, 1936–   II. Title.

PQ8498.32.A65E5613 2011
865'.64—dc22

                                                    2011003835

Designed by Jonathan D. Lippincott

www.fsgbooks.com

        1   3   5   7   9   10   8   6   4   2

IN PRAISE OF READING

AND FICTION

I LEARNED TO READ AT THE AGE OF FIVE, in Brother Justiniano's class at the De la Salle Academy in Cochabamba, Bolivia. It is the most important thing that has ever happened to me. Almost seventy years later, I remember clearly how the magic of translating the words in books into images enriched my life, breaking the barriers of time and space and allowing me to travel with Captain Nemo twenty thousand leagues under the sea, fight with d'Artagnan, Athos, Porthos, and Aramis against the intrigues threatening the queen in the days of the secretive Richelieu, or stumble through the sewers of Paris, transformed into Jean Valjean carrying Marius's inert body on my back.

Reading changed dreams into life and life into dreams and placed the universe of literature within reach of the boy I once was. My mother told me the first things I wrote were continuations of the stories I read because it made me sad when they concluded, or because I wanted to change their endings. And perhaps this is what I have spent my life doing without realizing it: prolonging in time, as I grew, matured, and aged, the stories that filled my childhood with exaltation and adventures.

I wish my mother were here, a woman who was moved to tears reading the poems of Amado Nervo and Pablo Neruda; and Grandfather Pedro too, with his large nose and gleaming bald head, who celebrated my verses; and Uncle Lucho, who urged me so energetically to throw myself body and soul into writing even though literature, in that time and place, compensated its devotees so badly. Throughout my life

I have had people like that at my side, people who loved and encouraged me and infected me with their faith when I had doubts. Thanks to them, and certainly to my obstinacy and some luck, I have been able to devote most of my time to the passion, the vice, the marvel of writing, creating a parallel life where we can take refuge against adversity, one that makes the extraordinary natural and the natural extraordinary, dissipates chaos, beautifies ugliness, eternalizes the moment, and turns death into a passing spectacle.

Writing stories was not easy. When they were turned into words, projects withered on the paper and ideas and images failed. How to reanimate them? Fortunately, the masters were there, teachers to learn from and examples to follow. Flaubert taught me that talent is unyielding discipline and long patience. Faulkner, that form—writing and structure—elevates or impoverishes subjects. Martorell, Cervantes, Dickens, Balzac, Tolstoy, Conrad, Thomas Mann, that scope and ambition are as important in a novel as stylistic dexterity and narrative strategy. Sartre, that words are acts, that a novel, a play, or an essay, engaged with the present moment and better options, can change the course of history. Camus and Orwell, that a literature stripped of morality is inhuman, and Malraux, that heroism and the epic are as possible in the present as in the time of the Argonauts, the *Odyssey*, and the *Iliad*.

If in this address I were to summon all the writers to whom I owe a few things or a great deal, their shadows would plunge us into darkness. They are innumerable. In addition to revealing the secrets of the storytelling craft, they obliged me to explore the bottomless depths of humanity, admire its heroic deeds, and feel horror at its savagery. They were my most obliging friends, the ones who vitalized my calling and in whose books I discovered that there is hope even in the worst of circumstances, that living is worth the effort if only because without life we could not read or imagine stories.

At times I wondered whether writing was not a solipsistic luxury in countries like mine, where there were so few readers, so many people who were poor and illiterate, so much injustice, and where culture was a privilege of the few. These doubts, however, never stifled my calling, and I always kept writing even during those periods when earning a living absorbed most of my time. I believe I did the right thing, since if, for literature to flourish, it was first necessary for a society to achieve high culture, freedom, prosperity, and justice, it never would have existed. But thanks to literature, to the consciousness it shapes, to the desires and longings it inspires, and to our disenchantment with reality when we return from the journey to a beautiful fantasy, civilization is now less cruel than when storytellers began to humanize life with their fables. We would be worse than we are without the good books we have read, more conformist, not as restless, more submissive, and the critical spirit, the engine of progress, would not even exist. Like writing, reading is a protest against the insufficiencies of life. When we look in fiction for what is missing in life, we are saying, with no need to say it or even to know it, that life as it is does not satisfy our thirst for the absolute—the foundation of the human condition—and should be better. We invent fictions in order to live in some way the many lives we would like to lead when we barely have one at our disposal.

Without fictions we would be less aware of the importance of freedom in making life livable, of the hell it turns into when it is trampled underfoot by a tyrant, an ideology, or a religion. Let those who doubt that literature not only submerges us in the dream of beauty and happiness but alerts us to every kind of oppression ask themselves why all regimes determined to control the behavior of citizens from cradle to grave fear it so much that they establish systems of censorship to repress it and keep so wary an eye on independent writers. They do this because they know the risk of allowing the imagination to wander free in books, know how fictions become seditious when the reader compares the freedom that makes them possible and is exercised in them with the obscurantism and fear lying in wait in the real world. Whether they want it or not, whether they know it or not, when they invent stories, the writers of tales propagate dissatisfaction, demonstrating that the world is badly made and the life of fantasy richer than the life of our daily routine. This fact, if it takes root in their sensibility and consciousness, makes citizens more difficult to manipulate, less willing to accept the lies of interrogators and jailers who would like to make them believe that behind bars they lead more secure and better lives.

Good literature erects bridges between different peoples, and by having us enjoy, suffer, or feel surprise, unites us beneath the languages, beliefs, habits, customs, and prejudices that separate us. When the great white whale buries Captain Ahab in the sea, the hearts of readers take fright in exactly the same way in Tokyo, Lima, or Timbuktu. When Emma Bovary swallows arsenic, Anna Karenina throws herself in front of the train, Julien Sorel climbs to the scaffold, and when, in "El sur," the urban doctor Juan Dahlmann walks out of that tavern on the pampa to face a thug's knife, or we realize that all the residents of Comala, Pedro Páramo's village, are dead, the shudder is the same in the reader who worships Buddha, Confucius, Christ, Allah, or is an agnostic, wears a jacket and tie, a djellaba, a kimono, or bombachas. Literature creates a fraternity within human diversity and eclipses the frontiers erected among men and women by ignorance, ideologies, religions, languages, and stupidity.

Since every period has its horrors, ours is the age of fanatics, of suicide terrorists, an ancient species convinced that by killing they earn heaven, that the blood of innocents washes away collective affronts, corrects injustices, and imposes truth on false beliefs. Every day, all over the world, countless victims are sacrificed by those who feel they possess absolute truth. With the collapse of totalitarian empires, we believed that coexistence, peace, pluralism, and human rights would gain the ascendancy and the world would leave behind holocausts, genocides, invasions, and wars of extermination. None of that has occurred. New forms of barbarism flourish, incited by fanaticism, and with the proliferation of weapons of mass destruction, we cannot overlook the fact that any small faction of crazed redeemers may one day provoke a nuclear cataclysm. We have to thwart them, confront them, and defeat them. They aren't many, although the tumult of their crimes resounds all over the planet and the nightmares they provoke overwhelm us with dread. We should not allow ourselves to be intimidated by those who want to snatch away the freedom we have been acquiring over the long course of civilization. Let us defend the liberal democracy that, with all its limitations, continues to signify political pluralism, co-existence, tolerance, human rights, respect for criticism, legality, free elections, alternation in power, everything that has been taking us out of a savage life and bringing us closer—though we will never attain it—to the beautiful, perfect life literature devises, the one we can deserve only by inventing, writing, and reading it. By confronting homicidal fanatics, we defend our right to dream and to make our dreams reality.

In my youth, like many writers of my generation, I was a Marxist and believed socialism would be the remedy for the exploitation and social injustices that were becoming more severe in my country, in Latin America, and in the rest of the Third World. My disillusion with statism and collectivism and my transition to the democrat and liberal that I am—that I try to be—was long and difficult and carried out slowly, a consequence of episodes like the conversion of the Cuban Revolution, about which I had initially been enthusiastic, to the authoritarian, vertical model of the Soviet Union; the testimony of dissidents who managed to slip past the barbed-wire fences of the Gulag; the invasion of Czechoslovakia by the nations of the Warsaw Pact; and because of thinkers like Raymond Aron, Jean-Francois Revel, Isaiah Berlin, and Karl Popper, to whom I owe my reevaluation of democratic culture and open societies. Those masters were an example of lucidity and gallant courage when the intelligentsia of the West, as a result of frivolity or opportunism, appeared to have succumbed to the spell of Soviet socialism or, even worse, to the bloody witches' Sabbath of the Chinese Cultural Revolution.

As a boy I dreamed of one day going to Paris because, dazzled by French literature, I believed that living there and breathing the air breathed by Balzac, Stendhal, Baudelaire, and Proust would help transform me into a real writer, and if I did not leave Peru, I would be only a pseudo, Sundays-and-holidays writer. And the truth is, I owe to France and French culture unforgettable lessons—for example, that literature is as much a calling as it is a discipline, a job, an obstinacy. I lived there when Sartre and Camus were alive and writing, the years of Ionesco, Beckett, Bataille, Cioran, the discovery of the theater of Brecht and the films of Ingmar Bergman, the Théâtre National Populaire of Jean Vilar and the Odéon of Jean-Louis Barrault, the Nouvelle Vague and the nouveau roman, the speeches—beautiful literary pieces—of André Malraux, and what may have been the most theatrical spectacle in Europe during that time, the press conferences and Olympic thunderings of General de Gaulle. But perhaps I am most grateful to France for the discovery of Latin

America. There I learned that Peru was part of a vast community united by history, geography, social and political problems, a certain mode of being, and the delicious language it spoke and wrote. And in those same years, it was producing a new, forceful literature. There I read Borges, Octavio Paz, Cortázar, García Márquez, Fuentes, Cabrera Infante, Rulfo, Onetti, Carpentier, Edwards, Donoso, and many others whose writings were revolutionizing narrative in the Spanish language, and thanks to whom Europe and a good part of the world discovered that Latin America was not the continent only of coups, operetta despots, bearded guerrillas, and the maracas of the mambo and the cha-cha, but of ideas, artistic forms, and literary fantasies that transcended the picturesque and spoke a universal language.

From that time to this, not without stumbling and blunders, Latin America has made progress, although, as César Vallejo said in a poem, *"Hay, hermanos, muchísimo que hacer"* ["There is still, brothers, so much to do"]. We are afflicted with fewer dictatorships than before: only Cuba and her named successor, Venezuela; and some pseudopopulist, clownish democracies like those in Bolivia and Nicaragua. But in the rest of the continent democracy is functioning, supported by a broad popular consensus, and for the first time in our history, as in Brazil, Chile, Uruguay, Peru, Colombia, the Dominican Republic, Mexico, and almost all of Central America, we have a left and a right that respect legality, the freedom to criticize, elections, and succession in power. That is the right road, and if we stay on it, combat insidious corruption, and continue to integrate with the world, Latin America will finally stop being the continent of the future and become the continent of the present.

I never felt like a foreigner in Europe or, in fact, anywhere. In all the places I have lived, in Paris, London, Barcelona, Madrid, Berlin, Washington, New York,

Brazil, or the Dominican Republic, I felt at home. I have always found a lair where I could live in peace, work, learn things, nurture dreams, and find friends, good books to read, and subjects to write about. It does not seem to me that my unintentionally becoming a citizen of the world has weakened what are called "my roots," my connections to my own country—which would not be particularly important—because if that were so, my Peruvian experiences would not continue to nourish me as a writer and would not always appear in my stories, even when they seem to occur very far from Peru. I believe, instead, that living for so long outside the country where I was born has strengthened those connections, adding a more lucid perspective to them, and a nostalgia that can differentiate the adjectival from the substantive and keep memories reverberating. Love of the country where one was born cannot be obligatory, but like any other love must be a spontaneous act of the heart, like the one that unites lovers, parents and children, and friends.

I carry Peru deep inside me because that is where I was born, grew up, was formed, and lived those experiences of childhood and youth that shaped my personality and forged my calling, and there I loved, hated, enjoyed, suffered, and dreamed. What happens there affects me more, moves and exasperates me more, than what occurs elsewhere. I have not wished it or imposed it on myself; it simply is so. Some compatriots accused me of being a traitor, and I was on the verge of losing my citizenship when, during the last dictatorship, I asked the democratic governments of the world to penalize the regime with diplomatic and economic sanctions, as I have always done with all dictatorships of any kind, whether of Pinochet, Fidel Castro, the Taliban in Afghanistan, the Imams in Iran, apartheid in South Africa, or the uniformed satraps of Burma (now called Myanmar). And I would do it again tomorrow if—may destiny not wish it and Peruvians not permit it—Peru were once again the victim of a coup that would annihilate our fragile democracy. It was not the precipitate, emotional action of a resentful man, as some scribblers wrote, accustomed to judging others from the point of view of their own pettiness. It was an act in line with my conviction that a dictatorship represents absolute evil for a country, a source of brutality and corruption and profound wounds that take a long time to close, poison the nation's future, and create pernicious habits and practices that endure for generations and delay democratic reconstruction. This is why dictatorships must be fought without hesitation, with all the means at our disposal, including economic sanctions. It is regrettable that democratic governments, instead of setting an example by making common cause with those, like the Damas de Blanco in Cuba, the Venezuelan opposition, or Aung San Suu Kyi and Liu Xiaobo, who courageously confront the dictatorships they endure, often show themselves accepting not of them but of their tormentors. Those valiant people, struggling for their freedom, are also struggling for ours.

A compatriot of mine, José María Arguedas, called Peru the country of "every blood." I do not believe any formula defines it better. That is what we are and that is what all Peruvians carry inside us, whether we like it or not: an aggregate of traditions, races, beliefs, and cultures proceeding from the four cardinal points. I am proud to feel myself the heir to the pre-Hispanic cultures that created the textiles and feather mantles of Nazca and Paracas, the Mochican or Incan ceramics exhibited in the best museums in the world, the builders of Machu Picchu, Gran Chimú, Chan Chan, Kuelap, Sipán, the burial grounds of El Brujo, El Sol, and La Luna, and to the Spanish who, with their saddlebags, swords, and horses, brought to Peru Greece, Rome, the Judeo-Christian tradition, the Renaissance, Cervantes,

Quevedo, and Góngora, and the harsh language of Castile, later sweetened in the Andes. And with Spain came Africa, with its strength, its music, and its effervescent imagination, to enrich Peruvian heterogeneity. If we investigate only a little we discover that Peru, like the Aleph of Borges, is a small format of the entire world. What an extraordinary privilege for a country not to have an identity because it has all of them!

The conquest of America was cruel and violent, like all conquests, of course, and we should criticize it but not forget as we do that those who committed pillage and crimes were, for the most part, our great-grandfathers and great-great-grandfathers, the Spanish who came to America and adopted American ways, not those who remained in their own country. Such criticism, to be just, should be self-criticism. Because when we gained our independence from Spain two hundred years ago, those who assumed power in the former colonies, instead of liberating the Indians and creating justice for old wrongs, continued exploiting them with as much greed and ferocity as the conquerors and, in some countries, decimating and exterminating them. Let us say this with absolute clarity: for two centuries the emancipation of the indigenous population has been our exclusive responsibility, and we have not fulfilled it. This continues to be an unresolved issue in all of Latin America. There is not a single exception to this ignominy and shame.

I love Spain as much as Peru, and my debt to her is as great as my gratitude. If not for Spain, I never would have reached this podium or become a known writer, and perhaps, like so many unfortunate colleagues, I would be wandering in the limbo of writers without luck, publishers, prizes, or readers, whose talent—sad comfort—posterity might one day discover. All my books were published in Spain, where I received exaggerated recognition, and where friends like Carlos Barral, Carmen

Balcells, and so many others were zealous about my stories having readers. And Spain granted me a second nationality at a time when I could have lost my first one. I have never felt the slightest incompatibility between being Peruvian and having a Spanish passport, because I have always felt that Spain and Peru are two sides of the same coin, not only in my small person but in essential realities like history, language, and culture.

Of all the years I have lived on Spanish soil, I remember as most brilliant the five I spent in a dearly loved Barcelona in the early 1970s. Franco's dictatorship was still in power and still shooting, but by then it was a fossil in rags, and, especially in the field of culture, incapable of maintaining its earlier controls. Cracks and chinks were opening that the censors could not patch over, and through them Spanish society absorbed new ideas, books, currents of thought, and artistic values and forms prohibited until then as subversive. No city took as much or better advantage of this start of an opening than Barcelona, or experienced a comparable excitement in all fields of ideas and creativity. It became the cultural capital of Spain, the place you had to be to breathe anticipation of the freedom to come. And, in a sense, it was also the cultural capital of Latin America, because of the number of painters, writers, publishers, and artists from Latin American countries who either settled in or traveled back and forth to Barcelona: it was where you had to be if you wanted to be a poet, novelist, painter, or composer in our time. For me, those were unforgettable years of comradeship, friendship, plots, and fertile intellectual work. Just as Paris had been, Barcelona was a Tower of Babel, a cosmopolitan, universal city where it was stimulating to live and work and where, for the first time since the days of the Civil War, Spanish and Latin American writers mixed and fraternized, recognizing one another as possessors of the same tradition and allied in a common enterprise and certainty: the end of the dictatorship was imminent, and, in democratic Spain, culture would be the principal protagonist.

Although it did not occur exactly that way, the Spanish transition from dictatorship to democracy has been one of the best stories of modern times, an example of how, when good sense and reason prevail and political adversaries set aside sectarianism for the common good, events can occur as marvelous as the ones in novels of magic realism. The Spanish transition from authoritarianism to freedom, from underdevelopment to prosperity, from Third World economic contrasts and inequalities to a country of middle classes, her integration into Europe, and her adoption in a few years of a democratic culture, have astonished the entire world and precipitated Spain's modernization. It has been moving and instructive for me to experience this near at hand, at times from the inside. I fervently hope that nationalism, the incurable plague of the modern world and of Spain as well, does not ruin this happy tale.

I despise every form of nationalism, a provincial ideology (or rather, religion) that is shortsighted and exclusive, that cuts off the intellectual horizon and hides in its bosom ethnic and racist prejudices, for it transforms into a supreme value, a moral and ontological privilege, the fortuitous circumstance of one's birthplace. Along with religion, nationalism has been the cause of the worst slaughters in history, like those in the two world wars and the current bloodletting in the Middle East. Nothing has contributed as much as nationalism to Latin America's having been Balkanized and stained with blood in senseless battles and disputes, squandering astronomical resources to purchase weapons instead of building schools, libraries, and hospitals.

We should not confuse a blinkered nationalism and its rejection of the Other, always the seed of violence, with patriotism, a salutary, generous feeling of love for the land where we were born, where our ancestors lived, where our first dreams were forged, a familiar landscape of geographies, loved ones, and events that are transformed into signposts of memory and defenses against solitude. Homeland is not flags, anthems, or apodictic speeches about emblematic heroes, but a handful of places and people that populate our memories and tinge them with melancholy, the warm sensation that no matter where we are, there is a home for us to return to.

Peru for me is Arequipa, where I was born but never lived, a city my mother, grandparents, and aunts and uncles taught me to know through their memories and yearnings, because my entire family tribe, as Arequepeños tend to do, always carried the White City with them in their wandering existence. It is the Piura of the desert, the mesquite trees and the long-suffering burros that Piurans of my youth called "somebody else's feet"—an elegant, sad name—where I discovered that storks did not bring babies into the world but couples made them by doing outrageous things that were a mortal sin. It is San Miguel Academy and the Varieties Theater, where for the first time I saw a short work I had written produced onstage. It is the corner of Diego Ferré and Colón, in Lima's Miraflores—we called it the Happy Neighborhood—where I exchanged short pants for long trousers, smoked my first cigarette, learned to dance, fall in love, and open my heart to girls. It is the dusty, pulsing editorial offices of the paper *La Crónica*, where, at sixteen, I stood vigil over my first youthful weapons as a journalist, a trade that, along with literature, has occupied almost my entire life and, like books, has made me live more, know the world better, and be with men and women from every place and every class—excellent, good, bad, and execrable people. It is the Leoncio Prado Military Academy, where I learned that Peru was not the small middle-class redoubt where I had lived until then, confined and protected, but a large, ancient, rancorous, unequal country, shaken by all kinds of social storms. It is the clandestine cells of Cahuide in which, with a handful of San Marcos students, we prepared the world revolution. And Peru is my friends in the Freedom Movement with whom for three years, in the midst of bombs, blackouts, and terrorist assassinations, I worked in defense of democracy and the culture of freedom.

Peru is Patricia, my cousin with the upturned nose and indomitable character, whom I was lucky enough to marry forty-five years ago and who still endures the manias, neuroses, and temper tantrums that help me to write. Without her my life would have dissolved a long time ago into a turbulent whirlwind, and Álvaro, Gonzalo, Morgana, and the six grandchildren who extend and gladden our existence would not have been born. She does everything and does everything well. She solves problems, manages our budget, imposes order on chaos, keeps journalists and intrusive people at bay, defends my time, determines appointments and trips, packs and unpacks suitcases, and is so generous that even when she thinks she is rebuking me, she pays me the highest compliment: "Mario, the only thing you're good for is writing."

Let us return to literature. The paradise of childhood is not a literary myth for me but a reality I lived and enjoyed in the large family house with three courtyards in Cochabamba, where, with my cousins and school friends, we could reproduce the stories of Tarzan and Salgari, and in the prefecture of Piura, where bats nested in the lofts, silent shadows that filled the starry nights of that hot land with mystery. During those years, writing was playing a game my family celebrated, something charming that earned applause for me, the grandson, the nephew, the son without a papa because my father had died and gone to heaven. He was a tall, good-looking man in a navy uniform whose photo, adorning my night table, I prayed to and then kissed before going to sleep. One Piuran morning—I do not think I have recovered from it yet—my mother revealed that the gentleman was, in fact, alive. And on that very day we were going to live with him in Lima. I was eleven years old, and from that moment everything changed. I lost my innocence and discovered loneliness, authority, adult life, and fear. My salvation was reading, reading good books, taking refuge in those worlds where life was glorious, intense, one adventure after another, where I could feel free and be happy again. And it was writing, in secret, like someone giving himself up to an unspeakable vice, a forbidden passion. Literature stopped being a game. It became a way of resisting adversity, protesting, rebelling, escaping the intolerable, my reason for living. From then until now, in every circumstance when I have felt disheartened or beaten down, on the edge of despair, giving myself body and soul to my work as a storyteller has been the light at the end of the tunnel, the plank that carries the shipwrecked man to shore.

Although it is very difficult and forces me to sweat blood and, like every writer, to feel at times the threat of paralysis, a dry season of the imagination, nothing has made me enjoy life as much as spending months and years constructing a story from its uncertain beginnings—the image stored by memory of a lived experience that becomes a restlessness, an enthusiasm, a daydream that then germinates into a project—and the decision to attempt to convert the agitated cloud of phantoms into a story. "Writing is a way of living," said Flaubert. Yes, absolutely, a way of living with illusion and joy and a fire throwing out sparks in your head, struggling with intractable words until you master them, exploring the broad world like a hunter tracking down desirable prey to feed an embryonic fiction and appease the voracious appetite of every story that, as it grows, would like to devour every other story. Beginning to feel the vertigo a gestating novel induces in us when it takes shape and seems to begin to live on its own, with characters that move, act, think, feel, and demand respect and consideration, on whom it is no longer possible to impose behavior arbitrarily or deprive of their free will without killing them or having the story lose its power to persuade—this is an experience that continues to bewitch me as it did the first time, as complete and dizzying as making love to the woman you love, for days, weeks, months, without stopping.

When speaking of fiction, I have talked a great deal about the novel and very little about the theater, another of its preeminent forms. A great injustice, of course. Theater was my first love, ever since, as an adolescent, I saw Arthur Miller's *Death of a Salesman* at the Segura Theater in Lima, a performance that left me transfixed with emotion and precipitated my writing a drama about Incas. If there had been a theatrical movement in the Lima of the 1950s, I would have been a playwright rather than a novelist. There was not, and that must have turned me more and more toward narrative. But my love for the theater never ended; it dozed, curled up in the shadow of novels, like a temptation and a nostalgia, above all whenever I saw an enthralling play. In the late 1970s, the persistent memory of a hundred-year-old great-aunt, Mamaé, who in the final years of her life cut off her surrounding reality to take refuge in memories and fiction, suggested a story. And I felt, prophetically, that it was a story for the theater, that only onstage would it take on the animation and splendor of successful fictions. I wrote it with the tremulous excitement of a beginner and so enjoyed seeing it with Norma Aleandro in the heroine's role that, since then, between novels and essays, I have relapsed several times. And I must add, I never imagined that at the age of seventy I would mount (I should say, stumble onto) a stage to act. That reckless adventure made me experience for the first time in my own flesh and bone the miracle it is for someone who has spent his life writing fictions to embody for a few hours a character of fantasy, to live the fiction in front of an audience. I can never adequately thank my dear friends, the director Joan Ollé and the actress Aitana Sánchez-Gijón, for having encouraged me to share with them that fantastic experience (in spite of the panic that accompanied it).

Literature is a false representation of life that nevertheless helps us to understand life better, to orient ourselves in the labyrinth where we are born, pass by, and die. It compensates for the reverses and frustrations real life inflicts on us, and because of it we can decipher, at least partially, the hieroglyphic that existence tends to be for the great majority of human beings, principally those of us who generate more doubts than certainties and confess our perplexity before subjects like transcendence, individual and collective destiny, the soul, the sense or senselessness of history, and the to-and-fro of rational knowledge.

I have always been fascinated to imagine the uncertain circumstance in which our ancestors—still barely different from animals, the language that allowed them to communicate with one another just recently born—in caves, around fires, on nights seething with the menace of lightning bolts, thunderclaps, and growling beasts, began to invent and tell stories. That was the crucial moment in our destiny, because in those circles of primitive beings held by the voice and fantasy of the storyteller civilization began—the long passage that gradually would humanize us and lead us to invent the autonomous individual, disengage him from the tribe, devise science, the arts, law, freedom, and finally scrutinize the innermost recesses of nature, the human body, space, and travel to the stars. Those tales, fables, myths, legends, which resounded for the first time like new music before listeners intimidated by the mysteries and perils of a world where everything was unknown and dangerous, must have been a cool bath, a quiet pool for those spirits always on the alert, for whom existence meant barely eating, taking shelter from the elements, killing, and fornicating. From the time they began to dream collectively, to share their dreams, instigated by storytellers, they ceased to be tied to the treadmill of survival, a vortex of brutalizing tasks, and their life became dream, pleasure, fantasy, and a revolutionary plan: to break out of confinement and change and improve, a struggle to appease the desires and ambitions that stirred imagined lives in them, and the curiosity to clear away the mysteries that filled their surroundings.

This never-interrupted process was enriched when writing was born and stories, in addition to being heard, could be read, achieving the permanence literature confers on them. That is why it must be repeated incessantly until new generations are convinced of it: fiction is more than an entertainment, more than an intellectual exercise that sharpens one's sensibility and awakens a critical spirit. It is an absolute necessity so that civilization continues to exist, renewing and preserving in us the best of what is human. So that we do not retreat into the savagery of isolation, and life is not reduced to the pragmatism of specialists who see things profoundly but ignore what surrounds, precedes, and continues those things. So that we do not move from being served by the machines we have invented into becoming their servants and slaves. And because a world without literature would be a world without desires or ideals or irreverence, a world of automatons deprived of what makes the human being really human: the capacity to move out of oneself and into another, into others, modeled with the clay of our dreams.

From the cave to the skyscraper, from the club to weapons of mass destruction, from the tautological life of the tribe to the era of globalization, the fictions of literature have multiplied human experiences, preventing us from succumbing to lethargy, self-absorption, resignation. Nothing has sown so much disquiet, so disturbed our imagination and our desires, as the life of lies we add, thanks to literature, to the one we have, so we can be protagonists in the great adventures, the great passions real life will never give us. The lies of literature become truths through us, the readers transformed, infected with longings and, because of fiction, permanently questioning a mediocre reality. Sorcery that offers us the hope of having what we do not have, being what we are not, acceding to that impossible existence where like pagan gods we feel mortal and eternal at the same time: literature introduces into our spirits nonconformity and rebellion, which are behind all the heroic deeds that have contributed to the reduction of violence in human relationships. Reducing violence, not ending it. Because ours will always be, fortunately, an unfinished story. That is why we have to continue dreaming, reading, and writing, the most effective way we have found to alleviate our mortal condition, to defeat the corrosion of time, and to transform the impossible into possibility.

Stockholm, December 7, 2010

Mario Vargas Llosa was awarded the Nobel Prize in Literature in 2010 "for his cartography of structures of power and his trenchant images of the individual's resistance, revolt, and defeat." Peru's foremost writer, he has been awarded the Cervantes Prize, the Spanish-speaking world's most distinguished literary honor, and the Jerusalem Prize. His many works include *The Feast of the Goat*, *The Bad Girl*, *Aunt Julia and the Scriptwriter*, *The War of the End of the World*, and *The Storyteller*. He lives in London.